A Correspondence

BETWEEN

JOHN STERLING

AND

RALPH WALDO EMERSON

KENNIKAT PRESS SCHOLARLY REPRINTS

Dr. Ralph Adams Brown, Senior Editor

Series on
LITERARY AMERICA IN THE NINETEENTH CENTURY
Under the General Editorial Supervision of
Dr. Walter Harding
University Professor, State University of New York

A Correspondence

BETWEEN

JOHN STERLING

AND

RALPH WALDO EMERSON

WITH A SKETCH OF
STERLING'S LIFE

BY
EDWARD WALDO EMERSON

KENNIKAT PRESS
Port Washington, N. Y./London

A CORRESPONDENCE BETWEEN JOHN STERLING
AND RALPH WALDO EMERSON

First published in 1897
Reissued in 1971 by Kennikat Press
Library of Congress Catalog Card No: 70-122649
ISBN 0-8046-1297-8

Manufactured in the United States of America

PREFATORY NOTE

It has seemed to me proper to introduce these letters with a short account of Sterling and his work, believing that neither Carlyle's "Life of Sterling" nor Archdeacon Hare's "Memoir" are read by many persons nowadays, and Sterling's own works are difficult to obtain.

Through the kind permission of Colonel John Barton Sterling of London I am enabled to use his father's letters.

EDWARD W. EMERSON.

Concord, *September*, 1897.

STERLING AND EMERSON

Then smiled *King Elf and answered, 'A long way wilt*
thou ride
To where unpeace and trouble and griefs of the soul abide,
Yea, unto the death at last, — yet surely shalt thou win
The help of many people, so have thy way herein.
Forsooth no more may we hold thee than the hazel-copse
may hold
The sun of the early morning which turneth it all to gold.'

SIGURD THE VOLSUNG, WILLIAM MORRIS.

JOHN STERLING

HOW much the world owes, how little it credits, to the Illuminators.
King Admetus had one of these nomi-
nally tending his herds for a time, but
who did more than this for him ; and the
story has been remembered the better
because it has been the fortune of many
men to fall in with one of the herdsman's
descendants. However dark the times
and unpromising the place, these sons of
the morning will appear, and their bright
parentage shows through life, for the
years let them alone. In Rome in her
decline Juvenal found this saving rem-
nant, and rightly told their lineage in the
verses,

" Juvenes queis arte benigna
Et meliore luto finxit præcordia Titan."

Blest youths, though few, whose hearts the God of Day
Fashioned with loving hand and from a nobler clay.

3

Where they have come, they have gilded
the day for those around, and warmed
their hearts, and made the dim way plain ;
and when they suddenly passed, a bright
twilight has remained, and the voice has
rung for life in the ears that once knew
it. And because the twilight does not
last, and the echo perishes with the ears
that heard it, and the gain of these lives
is of a kind less easily pointed out to the
common eye than if it had taken form
in " goods," or inventions, or institutions,
or even laurels, men often lament and
count such lives as lost.

In presenting the words of good cheer
that passed between John Sterling, the
poet, and a friend, never seen, beyond
the ocean, I wish to urge that here was
one whose nobility and sympathy illuminated in his short day the lives of his
friends ; and though he died before his
noon, leaving little lasting work, yet was
not the light lost, for the seemingly more

4

enduring work of his friends was done in a measure in its rays.

"Poor Sterling," — such is the ever recurring burden of Carlyle's tribute to his friend, which he seems to have been pricked into writing largely because Sterling's other loyal friend and biographer, Archdeacon Hare, who had loved and labored with him in the Church of England, deplored overmuch his throwing off its rule and vestments. Though Carlyle has no sympathy for Sterling's knightly efforts to help the exile and the slave, and for his apostolic labors among the poor of England, scouts his verses and makes light of his essays and romance, and ever chafes because this fine courser was not a mighty dray-horse like himself, — yes, sad and soured by physical ailments, he more than half blamed his brave friend for having the cruel and long disease through which he worked, even to his censor's admiration, — yet, in

5

spite of all, Carlyle's Life of Sterling
shows in every page that this man's short,
brave course lifted and illuminated all
about him, even that weary and sad-eyed
Jeremiah himself as he sat apart and
prophesied and lamented. One recoils
at much of Carlyle's expression in this
work, but, with all its blemish of pity
and Philistinism and pessimism, it stands
remarkable, a monument built by such
hands, — I will not say planned by such
a mind, for the mind protested; but
nevertheless the hands, obedient to the
spirit, built it with the best they could
bring in gratitude to helpful love whose
sunlight had reached an imprisoned soul.

John Sterling died half a century ago.
Little of what he wrote remains. His
fine Strafford, a Tragedy, is now hard
to obtain, and few people even know
Dædalus, the best of his poems. His
work is noble in thought and often in expression, as befitted a man who bravely
turned away from his Church, with all it

then meant of opportunity and vantage-
ground, saying simply to his pleading
friends, "No, I cannot lie for God."

I will briefly recall the few outward
events of Sterling's life. Born in 1806,
in the Island of Bute, of gentle Scotch
blood warmed and spiced by the sojourn
of his immediate forerunners in Ireland,
and his first years passed in Gaelic and
Cymrian lands, it is no wonder that the
growth of the young mind and spirit was
determined rather in the direction of bold
and free and fine imagination than along
paths of unremitting and faithful toil.
Moreover, he had that quick sympathy
and entire generosity which, as prompt-
ing to turn aside for others' interests,
do not favor the concentration of effort.
These and the other good traits of the
Celtic races, their unquestioning courage,
loyalty, gayety, eloquence, gave Sterling
his brilliancy, which was saved from the
faults that usually go with the artistic
temperament by a delicate conscience

and the controlling moral sense and prin-
ciple, the best Saxon heritage.

He did not undergo the time-honored
and Philistine methods of the great public schools, so prized as a foundation of
manhood and grammar for an English
gentleman. He did not need that rude
schooling; the fire and manhood were
there, and he took to letters by nature.
He studied with various tutors, and became a student at Cambridge. Here
he was a light in the brightest under-
graduate society of his day, among whom
were men destined to impress their generation. The best of these — Frederick
Maurice, John Trench, John Kemble,
Richard Monckton Milnes, Charles Bul-
ler, and others — were his friends. He
did not value the English university as it
was in his day.

After leaving the university, and after
some false starts like an attempt at reading law and a temporary secretaryship of
a sort of politico-commercial association,

he soon came to his natural destiny, a literary life, and of course gravitated to London, where his father, a man of spirit and ability, was already a power in the *Times* newspaper.

Sterling joined with Maurice in conducting *The Athenæum*. Its high tone was distinctive while Sterling was connected with it, says Archdeacon Hare; and of his literary first-fruits, Essays and Tales, many of them cast in a Greek mould, even Carlyle, mainly contemptuous of anything artistic, has to say that they are "singularly beautiful and attractive." "Everywhere the point of view adopted is a high and noble one, and the result worked out a result to be sympathized with, and accepted as far as it will go."

The outward life among the highest literary society in London, in which his fine, spirited personality soon gave him prominence, was much to his taste, but meanwhile his inner life was growing

richer with the days. The simple nobility of Arnold, the Master of Rugby, had
early interested him; even in

"Streaming London's central roar"

the voice of Wordsworth from the West-
moreland hills reached him, created a
calm, and brought happiness; above all,
Coleridge, incomprehensible save to a
few, and now growing dim in age, but
to Sterling's eager soul illuminating the
mists in which he lived, became a power
in his life. Indeed, of some of his own
Athenæum papers Sterling modestly
wrote that he was "but a patch of sand
to receive and retain the Master's foot-
print." The gospel of the low place of
the understanding, and of faith as the
highest reason, lighted on their way the
disciples of this high priest strangely
arisen in the England of that day.

Sterling's youthful chivalry led him to
befriend and help the Spanish political
refugees, of whom a numerous band were
in London. Among others, he inter-

ested in this cause an adventurous young
kinsman, lately resigned from the army,
and keen for some daring enterprise,
and, with the means and zeal which this
ally brought, a descent on the coast of
Spain, to raise the revolutionary standard there, was planned. Sterling for-
warded this scheme as he could, and
meant personally to share in it, but was
dissuaded because of ill health and his
recent engagement of marriage. The
vessel was seized at the point of rendez-
vous on the Thames, the day before it
was to sail, with Sterling on board help-
ing in the preparations. He escaped
with cool audacity, warned the adventur-
ers, saved them from capture, and got
the now sorely crippled and disarmed ex-
pedition otherwise started. But disaster
dogged it, and after some tedious and in-
effectual attempts to promote a rising,
General Torrijos and his helpers, including Sterling's young relative, were cap-
tured, and summarily shot on the plaza

of Malaga. Because he had aided the rash venture, but had not shared its dangers, the blow was almost overwhelming to a man of Sterling's high honor, and it was a subject that could never be spoken of in his presence.

Before the final blow came, he had gone, because of alarming lung threatenings, to assume the care of an inherited family property in the Isle of St. Vincent, in the West Indies, carrying his young wife with him. There he met slavery, and, sharing the responsibility for it, began to consider, with both conscience and common sense, what could be done for the poor degraded bondsmen ; but his residence there was short, only fifteen months, and his improved health seemed to warrant an ending of this exile, so he returned to England in 1832. Though his genius called him to other works than professed philanthropy, and these and all of his works had to be done as they might with the sword of

Azrael hanging over him, — wounding him grievously many times before its final fall, — he did not forget the slaves, and hoped he might yet serve their cause.

To introduce a contrast which may be interesting, I quote Carlyle's views on this hope of Sterling's : —

"During the summer of 1832 I find traces of attempts towards anti-slavery philanthropy ; shadows of extensive schemes in that direction; half-desperate outlooks, it is likely, towards the refuge of philanthropism as a new chivalry of life. These took no serious hold of so clear an intellect, but they hovered now and afterwards as day dreams when life otherwise was shorn of aim : mirages in the desert, which are found not to be lakes when you put your bucket into them. . . . The sojourn at St. Vincent's was not to last much longer. Perhaps one might get some scheme raised into life in Downing Street for universal education of the blacks preparatory to emancipating them. There were a noble work for a man!"

February, 1835. "We talked rapidly of various unmemorable things. I remember coming on the negroes, and noticing that Sterling's notions on the Anti-slavery question had not advanced into the stage of mine. In reference to the question whether an 'engagement for life' on just terms between parties who are fixed in the character of master and servant, as the whites and negroes are, is not really better than one from day to day, he said with a kindly jeer, 'I would have the negroes themselves consulted as to that,' and would not in the least believe that the negroes were by no means final or perfect judges of it. His address, I perceived, was abrupt, unceremonious, etc.," — as might have been imagined.

Once more at home in England, and rejoicing in this, and yet more in the

blessing of wife and child, Sterling, now
maturing with richer experience, desiring
to serve his kind, and with new hope and
faith, essayed his hand in a thoughtful
novel, *Arthur Coningsby*, in which he
tried to show that the Church might
still have life and help hidden under its
externals. In this serious frame of mind
he chanced to meet his friend, Julius
Hare, a good man and a servant of the
Lord in the Church of England, who
well knew the nobility that lay in Sterling; and soon after he became Hare's
curate at Herstmonceux, in Sussex.

Into the high and the lowly duties of
his calling Sterling threw himself with
the zeal of the loved disciple, during the
few months that his health allowed him
to labor; though the zealous Paul was
rather his model, he said, and the village
cottages were to be to him his Derbe
and Lystra and Ephesus, a place where
he would bend his whole being, and
spend his heart for the conversion, puri-

fication, elevation, of the humble souls
therein. In that time he found much
happiness, and blessings followed his
steps in the village. But his physicians
told him that he could not do this work
and live, so with much regret he left the
post in which he had given such promise
of being helpful. It was a station on
his journey, a phase in his life; but he
passed on, and soon his growing spirit
found itself cramped by walls built for
men of other centuries and other stat-
ure. Yet for the remaining years of his
maimed and interrupted life he was a
noble soldier of the Church militant and
universal, a helper and a light.

Through ten years, with his life in his
hands, under continual marching orders,
cruelly separating him from his loved
and loyal wife and little children, to Madeira, Bordeaux, the southern towns of
England, and finally the Isle of Wight,
he never lost courage or faith, and worked
while yet there was day for him. And

though long disease wore out the body,
it could never touch his soul.

Sterling and Emerson never met face
to face, but there was so strong a likeness in some part of their lives — both
the events and the spiritual experience
and growth — that their friendship
seemed ordained above. Both men,
born with a commanding call to letters;
brought under the awakening influences
that moved England, Old and New, in
their generation ; helped first by Coleridge and charmed by Wordsworth, earnestly hoped to serve their fellow men
by living work in the Church in which
they found themselves, though it seemed
well-nigh lifeless then. Both, after a
short service, found their growth resisted
by the walls around them, and at once
passed fearlessly out of the Church par-
tial to be workers in the Church universal. Disease added its burden to each
at this time, and was bravely borne.

The words of Carlyle came to them,
and moved them so strongly that each
stretched a joyful and grateful hand to
him at a time when it seemed as if none
heeded ; and this their service to his soul
bound him for life to them, though his
sad and stormy spirit chafed at their
singing and chided their hope. Brought
into relation with each other by him,
they met in their honor for him, and in
that other part of their lives to which he
was deaf and blind, — their yearning to
express their respective messages in lasting verse ; and in this especially, in the
five short years of their friendship, their
hands, held out across the sea to each
other, gave to both happiness and help.

In Mr. Emerson's journal for the year
1843 is written the following pleasant
account of the coming together, along
lines of sympathy, of Sterling's life and
his own : —

"In Roxbury, in 1825, I read Cotton's

translation of Montaigne. It seemed to
me as if I had written the book myself
in some former life, so sincerely it spoke
my thought and experience. No book
before or since was ever so much to me
as that. How I delighted afterwards in
reading Cotton's dedication to Halifax,
and the reply of Halifax, which seemed
no words of course, but genuine suf-
frages. Afterwards I went to Paris in
1833, and to the Père la Chaise and
stumbled on the tomb of ———,[1] who, said
the stone, formed himself to virtue on
the Essays of Montaigne. Afterwards,
John Sterling wrote a loving criticism on
Montaigne in the *Westminster Review*,
with a journal of his own pilgrimage to
Montaigne's estate and château; and soon
after Carlyle writes me word that this

[1] Left blank in the journal, but in his volume *Representative Men*, in the chapter " Montaigne, or the Skeptic," he
writes : " In the Père la Chaise I came to the tomb of Au-
guste Collignon, who died in 1830, aged sixty-eight years,
and who, said the monument, 'lived to do right and had
formed himself to virtue on the Essays of Montaigne.' "

same lover of Montaigne is a lover of
me. Now I have been introducing to
his genius two of my friends, James and
Tappan, who both warm to him as to
their brother. So true is S. G. W.'s
saying that all whom he knew, met."

Here is the passage in the letter of
Carlyle above alluded to, written from
Chelsea, on the 8th of December, 1837:

"There is a man here called John
Sterling (*Reverend* John of the Church
of England too), whom I love better than
anybody I have met with, since a certain
sky-messenger alighted to me at Craigen-
puttock, and vanished in the Blue again.
This Sterling has written ; but what is
far better, he has lived, he is alive.
Across several unsuitable wrappages, of
Church-of-Englandism and others, my
heart loves the man. He is one, and the
best, of a small class extant here, who,
nigh drowning in a black wreck of Infi-
delity (lighted up by some glare of Radi-
calism only, now growing *dim*, too) and

about to perish, saved themselves into a Coleridgian Shovel-hattedness, or determination to *preach*, to preach peace, were it only the spent *echo* of a peace once preached. He is still only about thirty ; young ; and I think will shed the shovel-hat yet, perhaps. Do you ever read *Blackwood?* This John Sterling is the 'New Contributor' whom Wilson makes such a rout about, in the November and prior month : " Crystals from a Cavern, etc.," which it is well worth your while to see. Well, and what then, cry you? Why, then, this John Sterling has fallen overhead in love with a certain Waldo Emerson, — that is all. He saw the little Book Nature lying here ; and, across a whole *silva silvarum* of prejudices, discerned what was in it ; took it to his heart, — and indeed into his pocket ; and has carried it off to Madeira with him, whither, unhappily (though now with good hope and expectation), the Doctors have ordered him. This is the small

piece of pleasant news : that two sky-
messengers (such they were both of them
to me) have met and recognized each
other ; and by God's blessing there shall
one day be a trio of us; call you that
nothing ? "

The news of this new friend and fellow worker was joyfully welcomed by
Emerson in his answer. After reading
the prose and verse in *Blackwood*, he
says, " I saw that my man had a head
and a heart, and spent an hour or two
very happily in spelling his biography
out of his own hand, a species of palmis-
try in which I have a perfect reliance."
The letters to Carlyle written during the
next year and a half tell of his growing
interest in the man and his writings.

Carlyle's letter from Ecclefechan in
September, 1839, shows that the fated
friends are drawing near to one another :

" God speed you, my Brother. I hope
all good things of you; and wonder
whether, like Phœbus Apollo, you are

destined to be a youth forever. Sterling will be right glad to hear your praises ; not unmerited, for he is a man among millions, that John of mine, though his perpetual-mobility wears me out at times. Did he ever write to you ? His latest speculation was that he should and would ; but I fancy it is among the clouds again. I heard from him the other day, out of Welsh villages where he passed his boyhood, etc., all in a flow of 'lyrical recognition,' hope, faith, and sanguine unrest ; I have even some thoughts of returning by Bristol (in a week or so, that must be), and seeing him. The dog has been reviewing me, he says, and it is coming out in the next *Westminster !* He hates terribly my doctrine of ' *Silence.*' "

Emerson had sent to Sterling at various times, through the hands of their friend Carlyle, his orations, The American Scholar and Literary Ethics, delivered respectively before the Phi Beta

Kappa Society at Harvard University, August 31, 1837, and the literary societies at Dartmouth College, July 24, 1838; and probably also his Address to the Senior Class at the Divinity School at Cambridge. These cumulative gifts drew from Sterling the first letter of a series which, through the courtesy of Colonel John Barton Sterling of London, I am permitted to publish, together with Emerson's letters in reply.

24

THE CORRESPONDENCE

CLIFTON, *September 30, 1839.*

MY DEAR SIR, — It is a horrible effort to do at last what one ought to have done long ago, were it not still more horrible to postpone it longer. But having a conscience, or something nameless that does the work of one, I feel it some consolation that I have wronged myself most by my silence, and especially if I have let you suppose me insensible to the beauty and worth of the discourses you sent me, and to the still more valuable kindness which led you to favour me with them. Unhappily, I am a man of ill health and many petty concerns, of much locomotion and infinite laziness and procrastination ; and though my failures towards you are infinite, they are, if pos-

25

sible, more than infinite to my other friends, — not better, but of longer standing, and whose claims have therefore increased at compound interest to be still more serious than yours. One of the worst results of my neglect is that I can no longer offer you, in return for your books, the first vivid impressions which they made on me. I shall only now say that I have read very, very little modern English writing that has struck and pleased me so much; among recent productions, almost only those of our friend Carlyle, whose shaggy-browed and deep-eyed thoughts have often a likeness to yours which is very attractive and impressive, neither evidently being the double of the other. You must be glad to find him so rapidly and strongly rising into fame and authority among us. It is evident to me that his suggestions work more deeply into the minds of men in this country than those of any living man : work, not mining to draw forth riches, but tunnelling to carry inwards the light and air of the region from which he starts. I rejoice to learn from him that you are about to publish something more considerable, at least in bulk, than what I have hitherto seen of yours. I trust you will long continue to diffuse, by your example as well as doctrine, the knowledge that the Sun and Earth and Plato and Shakespeare are what they are by working each in his vocation; and that we can be anything better than mountebanks living, and scarecrows dead, only by doing so likewise. For my better assurance of this truth, as well as for much and cordial kindness, I shall always remain your debtor, and also,

Most sincerely yours,

JOHN STERLING.

II. EMERSON TO STERLING.

CONCORD, MASS., *29th May*, 1840.

MY DEAR SIR, — I have trusted your magnanimity to a good extent in neglecting to acknowledge your letter, received in the winter, which gave me great joy, and more lately your volume of poems, which I have had for some weeks. But I am a worshipper of Friendship, and cannot find any other good equal to it. As soon as any man pronounces the words which approve him fit for that great office, I make no haste: he is holy; let me be holy also; our relations are eternal; why should we count days and weeks? I had this feeling in reading your paper on Carlyle, in which I admired the rare behaviour, with far less heed the things said; these were opinions, but the tone was the man.[1] But I owe to you also the ordinary debts we

[1] In writing to Carlyle himself Emerson said, "I delighted in the spirit of that paper, — loving you so well, and accusing you so conscientiously."

In Carlyle's *Life of Sterling*, Part II. Cap. ii., it is hard to tell which to admire more, Sterling's just criticism, so bravely yet kindly expressed, of Carlyle's (Teufelsdröckh's) attitude to the universe, or the simple and friendly way in which Carlyle presents it, uncombated, to his readers.

incur to art. I have read these poems, and those, still more recent, in Blackwood, with great pleasure. The ballad of Alfred,[1] delighted me when I first read it, but I read it so often to my friends that I discovered that the last verses were not equal to the rest. Shall I gossip on and tell you that the two lines,

> " Still lives the song though Regnar dies !
> Fill high your cups again,"

rung for a long time in my ear, and had a kind of witchcraft for my fancy? I confess I am a little subject to these aberrations. The Sexton's Daughter is a gift to us all, and I hear allusions to it and quotations from it passing into common speech, which must needs gratify you. My wife insists that I shall tell you that she rejoices greatly that the man is in the world who wrote this poem. The Aphrodite is very agreeable to me, and I was sorry to miss the Sap-

1 *Alfred the Harper*, included later in Emerson's *Parnassus*.

pho from the Onyx Ring. I believe
I do not set an equal value on all the
pieces, yet I must count him happy who
has this delirious music in his brain, who
can strike the chords of Rhyme with a
brave and true stroke; for thus only do
words mount to their right greatness,
and airy syllables initiate us into the har-
monies and secrets of universal nature.
I am naturally keenly susceptible of the
pleasures of rhythm, and cannot believe
but that one day — I ask not where or
when — I shall attain to the speech of
this splendid dialect, so ardent is my
wish ; and these wishes, I suppose, are
ever only the buds of power ; but up to
this hour I have never had a true success in such attempts. My joy in any
other man's success is unmixed. I wish
you may proceed to bolder, to the best
and grandest melodies whereof your heart
has dreamed. I hear with some anxiety
of your ill health and repeated voyages.

Yet Carlyle tells me that you are not in danger. We shall learn one day how to prevent these perils of disease, or to look at them with the serenity of insight. It seems to me that so great a task is imposed on the young men of this generation that life and health have a new value. The problems of reform are losing their local and sectarian character, and becoming generous, profound, and poetic. If, as would seem, you are theoretically as well as actually somewhat a traveller, I wish America might attract you. The way is shorter every year, and the object more worthy. There are three or four persons in this country whom I could heartily wish to show to three or four persons in yours, and when I shall arrange any such interviews under my own roof I shall be proud and happy.

Your affectionate servant,

R. WALDO EMERSON.

THE CORRESPONDENCE

CLIFTON NEAR BRISTOL, *July* 18, 1840.

MY DEAR FRIEND, — Your cordial letter is the pleasantest of transatlantic greetings, and reminds me of the delight with which Columbus breathed the air and saw the flowers of his New World, which, though I have not discovered either it or anything, salutes me through you as kindly as if I too had launched caravels and lighted on new Indies. And so, in a sense, I have. Treasures and spice islands of good will and sympathy blow their airs to me from your dim poetic distance. In fancy I ride the winged horse you send me, to visit you in return, and though prosaic and hodiernal here, dream that I live an endless life of song and true friendly communion on the other side of the great water. In truth, literature has procured not one other such gratification as your letter gives me. Every other friend

I have — and I am not unfurnished with good and wise ones — I owe to outward circumstances and personal intercourse, and I believe you are the only man in the world that has ever found any printed words of mine at all decidedly pleasant or profitable. I heartily thank you for telling me the fact, and also for the fact itself. There are probably at least fifty persons in England who can write better poetry than mine, but I confess it pleases me very much that, independently of comparisons, you should see in it the thought and feeling which I meant to express, in words that few except yourself have perceived to be anything but jingle.

I have lately read with much satisfaction an American poem called What-Cheer,[1] which you probably know. Why did not the writer take a little more

---

[1] *What-Cheer, or Roger Williams in Banishment*, by Job Durfee, LL. D., Chief Justice of Rhode Island, published in 1832, and later in his Works in 1849.

pains ? It is more like my notion of a real American epic on a small scale than anything I had before imagined. With us poetry does not flourish. Hartley Coleridge, Alfred Tennyson, and Henry Taylor are the only younger men I now think of who have shown anything like genius, and the last — perhaps the most remarkable — has more of volition and understanding than imagination. Milnes and Trench are friends of mine, — as Taylor is, — but their powers are rather fine than truly creative. Carlyle, with all the vehement prejudice that becomes a prophet, is the great man arisen in later years among us, and is daily more and more widely felt, rather than understood, to be so. I have just come from London, where I saw a good deal of him during the five or six days I was there. He is writing down his last course of lectures, and will no doubt publish them. You will be amused by the clever and instructed obtuseness of the criticism on him in the Edinburgh Review, by I know not whom. I was very near going to America by the Great Western, a few days ago, to take care of a sister-in-law bound for Canada, where her husband, my brother, is. I should have paid you a visit inevitably. . . .

My wife greets you and yours, as my children would, were they sufficiently enlightened. The doctors have made me dawdle myself away remedially, and perchance irremediably, into a most unprofitable *eidolon*. Revive me soon with a book of yours, and believe me faithfully and gratefully yours,

JOHN STERLING.

IV. EMERSON TO STERLING.

CONCORD, 31*st March*, 1841.

MY DEAR SIR, — You gave me great content by a letter last summer, which I did not answer, thinking that shortly I should have a book to send you; but I am very slow, and my Essays, printed at last, are not yet a fortnight old. I have written your name in a copy, and sent it to Carlyle by the same steamer which should carry this letter. I wish, but scarce dare hope, you may find in it anything of the pristine sacredness of thought. All thoughts are holy when they come floating up to us in magical newness from the hidden Life, and 't is no wonder we are enamoured and love-sick with these Muses and Graces, until, in our devotion to particular beauties and in our efforts at artificial disposition, we lose somewhat of our universal sense and the sovereign eye of Proportion. All sins, literary and æsthetic and scientific, as well as moral, grow out of unbelief at last. We must needs meddle ambitiously, and cannot quite trust that there is life, self-evolving and indestructible, but which cannot be hastened, at the heart of every physical and metaphysical fact. Yet how we thank and greet, almost adore, the person who has once or twice

36

in a lifetime treated anything sublimely, and certified us that he beheld the Law! The silence and obscurity in which he acted are of no account, for everything is equally related to the soul.

I certainly did not mean, when I took up this paper, to write an essay on Faith, and yet I am always willing to declare how indigent I think our poetry and all literature is become for want of that. My thought had only this scope, no more: that though I had long ago grown extremely discontented with my little book, yet were the thoughts in it honest in their first rising, and honestly reported, but that I am very sensible how much in this, as in very much greater matters, interference, or what we miscall art, will spoil true things.[1] . . .

[1] In a letter to a friend (William Coningham), written June 20, 1841, Sterling says: " The only book of any pith and significance that has dawned here lately is a volume of Emerson's *Essays*, which, at a glance, seem far ahead in compass and brilliancy of almost everything England has of late years (generations) produced. In the rhetorical

I know not what sin of mine averted from you so good a purpose as to come to Canada and New England. Will not the brother leave the sister to be brought again? We have some beautiful and excellent persons here, to whom I long to introduce you and Carlyle, and our houses now stand so near that we must meet soon.

Your affectionate servant,

R. W. EMERSON.

I have left for my Postscript what

form with which he clothes his philosophy he resembles a little Schleiermacher in the beautiful *Reden*, and some of Schelling's early works — Schellingian mostly in spirit — a traveller that is on air-cleaving pinions, in the high regions of ontology. Greek philosophy in its earlier period had a good deal of this semi-poetic impulse and colouring, and we find it both in the East and in the writings of the mystics of the Middle Ages. It appears to me, in Emerson, perfectly genuine, as also in Novalis (whom he a little resembles), and in both it marks, I think, the great fact that ours is an age of germination and productive revolution, in which truth that has so long outlived its overworn and too narrow [. . .] starts out with a new force for an untried [. . .], and shows, faintly as yet and very doubtfully, the glow and freshness of youthful hope."

Letters to a Friend, by John Sterling, 1848.

should else be the subject of a new letter. A very worthy friend of mine, bred
a scholar at Cambridge, but now an iron-
manufacturer in this State, named ——,
writes me to request that I will ask you
for a correct list of your printed pieces,
prose and verse. He loves them very
much, and wishes to print them at Boston : he does not know how far our taste
will go, but he even hopes to realize
some pecuniary profit from the Phœni-
cians, which he will eagerly appropriate
to your benefit. Send me, I entreat, a
swift reply.

V. STERLING TO EMERSON.

PENZANCE, *April* 30, 1841.

MY DEAR SIR, — It is nearly a fortnight since the receipt of your welcome
letter of March 31, in which you were
good enough to express a wish for a
speedy reply. The state of my health
has, however, been such as to excuse
some delay ; and, moreover, during this

very time I have been employed in seeking for a house somewhere in these western regions of ours, as near as possible to America, finding it impossible to live longer in the dry, sharp, dogmatic air of Clifton. At last I have made a bargain for a dwelling at Falmouth. My family will probably be removing in June, and until then it may be feared that I shall have but little quiet for any of the better ends of life, which indeed the frailty of my health in a great degree withdraws me from. One of the disadvantages of our future abode is the remoteness from London, which produces many inconveniences, and among others delay and difficulty in procuring books. Even now I feel the mischief in the want of the copy of your Essays which your kindness designed for me. I console myself by reflecting that I have a hid treasure which will come to light some day. There are at this hour, in the world, so far as I know, just three persons writing English who attempt

to support human nature on anything better than arbitrary dogmas or hesitating
negations. These are Wordsworth, Carlyle, and you. The practical effect, however, of Wordsworth's genius, though not
of course its intrinsic value, is much di-
minished by the extreme to which he
carries the expedient of compromise and
reserve; and the same was even more
true of my dear and honoured friend Coleridge. Neither Carlyle nor you can be
charged with such timidity, and I look for
the noblest and most lasting fruits from
the writings of both, to say nothing of
the profit and delight which they yield
to me personally, who am already at one
with those friends on many points that
most divide them from their contemporaries. Nothing seems more difficult than
to ascertain what extent of influence such
work as yours and his are gaining among
us, but in my boyhood, twenty years ago,
I well remember that, with quite insignifi-
cant exceptions, all the active and daring

minds which would not take for granted the Thirty-Nine Articles and the Quarterly Review took refuge with teachers like Mackintosh and Jeffrey, or at highest Madame de Staël. Wordsworth and Coleridge were mystagogues lurking in caverns, and German literature was thought of with a good deal less favour than we are now disposed to show towards that of China. Remembering these things, and seeing the revolution accomplished among a part of the most instructed class and affecting them all, and also the blind, drunken movements of awakening intelligence among the labourers, which have succeeded to their former stupid sleep, one can hardly help believing that as much energetic and beneficial change has taken place among us during the last quarter of a century as at any former period during the same length of time.

As to me, I certainly often have fancied that, with longer intervals of health, I might be a fellow worker with you and

the one or two others whose enterprise
has alone among all the projects round
us at once high worth and solid perma-
nence. But the gods have this matter
in their hands, and I have long discovered that it is too large for mine. Lat-
terly I have been working at a tragedy,
but with many intimations that my own
catastrophe might come before that of
my hero. It may perhaps be possible to
complete the tangled net before the next
winter weaves its frostwork among the
figures and numbs the workman's hand.

Mr. ——, whom you wrote of, deserves
and has all my thanks. It is a true
sunny pleasure, worth more than all medi-
cine, to know of any one man in the world
who sees what one means, and cares for
it, and does not regard one's heart's blood
as so much puddle water. It would be a
great satisfaction to me to have my things
reprinted as a whole in America.

.   .   .   .

Forgive this random gossip, and the

43

emptiness of a letter which ought to have expressed much better how truly and affectionately I am yours,

JOHN STERLING.

VI. STERLING TO EMERSON.

FALMOUTH, *December 28th*, 1841.

MY DEAR FRIEND, — Your Oration of the 11th August [1] has only just reached me. Pray accept my thanks for it. Without this new mark of your kind recollection I should have written to you at this time, for, after much work and much illness, I have been looking forward to the end of the year as a time when the last twelvemonth might be pleasantly rounded off with letters to several friends for a long while past too much neglected. These are mostly persons with whom I have once been in more familiar intercourse than at present; years and saddening experiences and local remoteness

---

[1] *The Method of Nature*, delivered before the Society of the Adelphi in Waterville College, Maine.

44

having a good deal divided me of late from most of my former Cambridge and London intimates. You are the only man in the world with whom, though unseen, I feel any sort of nearness; all my other cordialities having grown up in the usual way of personal intercourse. This sort of anomalous friendship is owing, I think, even more to your letters than to your books, which, however, are always near my hand. The Essays I have just read over again, with new and great pleasure. It also often occurs to me to look back with joy at the kindness you have expressed in writing to me, and to say, after all, our clay has been mixed with something happier than tears and blood; for there is a man beyond the Atlantic whom I never saw, and who yet is to me a true and understanding friend. By the way, your Essays on Love and Friendship are to me perhaps more delightful than anything you have written. In this last Oration there is much that I feel strongly;

much, also, that makes me speculate on the kind of Church or Public that you address, — which must be very unlike anything among us ; much, again, which does not find me, — specially that abnegation of individualism which has become less possible for me as I have gone on in life, and which, by the way, is perhaps the most striking doctrinal difference between you and Carlyle. As to your audience or church, I doubt whether there are anywhere in Britain, except in London, a hundred persons to be found capable of at all appreciating what seems to find, as spoken by you, such ready acceptance from various bodies of learners in America. Here we have not only the same aggressive material element as in the United States, but a second fact unknown there, namely, the social authority of Church Orthodoxy, derived from the close connection between the Aristocracy (that is, the Rich) and the Clergy. And odd it is to see that, so

46

far as appears on the surface, the last twenty-five years have produced *more* of this instead of less.

Incomparably our most hopeful phenomenon is the acceptance of Carlyle's writings. But how remarkable it is that the critical and historical difficulties of the Bible were pointed out by clear-sighted English writers more than a century ago, and thence passed through Voltaire into the whole mind of Continental Europe, and yet that in this country both the facts and the books about them remain utterly unknown except to a few recluses ! The overthrow of our dead Biblical Dogmatism must, however, be preparing, and may be nearer than appears. The great curse is the wretched and seemingly hopeless mechanical pedantry of our Monastic Colleges at Oxford and Cambridge. I know not whether there is much connection between these things and the singular fact, I believe quite unexampled in England for three hundred years, that there is no man living among us, — literally, I believe, not one, — under the age of fifty, whose verses will pay the expense of publication. Nevertheless I have been working in that way, remembering what Cornelius, the German, the greatest of modern painters, said lately in London, — that he and Overbeck were obliged to starve for twenty years, and then became famous.

I am far from having forgotten my promise to you to examine and revise all my past writings. But I find little that I am at present at all prepared to reprint. The verses I have carefully corrected, and these would form a volume about the size of the last. But as only about a hundred copies of that have been sold, I dare not propose printing any more, even under favour of my kind and munificent friend the Iron Master, to whom and to you I hope to be able to send soon Strafford, a Tragedy, in print. It has cost me many months of hard work,

and I have some hope of finding a bookseller rash enough to print it. It is *possible* that I may see you early in summer,
as there seems a chance of my having
to go on business to St. Vincent, and I
would try to take you and Niagara on
my way home.

Believe me your affectionate

JOHN STERLING.

VII. EMERSON TO STERLING.

CONCORD, 1*st April*, 1842.

MY DEAR SIR, — I will not reckon
how many weeks and months I have let
pass since I received from you a letter
which greatly refreshed me, both by its
tone and its matter. Since that time I
have been sorely wounded, utterly im-
poverished, by the loss of my only son, a
noble child a little more than five years
old, and in these days must beguile my
poverty and nakedness as I can, by books
and studies which are only a diversion;
for it is only oblivion, not consolation,

that such a calamity can admit, whilst it is new.

You do not in your letter distinctly say that you will presently send me with the Tragedy of Strafford, which I look for, the promised list of prose and verse for Mr. ———. Yet you must; for I read a few weeks ago, in a Southern newspaper, the proposals of a Philadelphia bookseller to print all your poems. I wrote immediately to the person named as editor in the advertisement, to inform him of our project and correspondence with you, and of the Tragedy that should come; and as I have heard nothing further, I presume that he has desisted. So far, then, his movement is only a good symptom, and should engage you to send the list, with such errata or revisions as you have, with the Strafford, to which may the Muse grant the highest success, the noblest conclusion.

I read with great pleasure that perhaps you will come to New England this ensu-

ing summer. Come, and bring your scroll
in your hand. Come to Boston and Concord, and I will go to Niagara with you.
I have never been there ; I think I will
go. I am quite sure that, to a pair of
friendly, poetic English eyes, I could so
interpret our political, social, and spiritual picture here in Massachusetts that
it should be well worth study as a table
of comparison. And yet perhaps, much
more than the large pictures, I fancy
that I could engage your interest in the
vignettes and pendants. However, about
this time, or perhaps a few weeks later,
we shall send you a large piece of spiritual New England, in the shape of A.
Bronson Alcott, who is to sail for London about the 20th April, and whom you
must not fail to see, if you can compass
it. A man who cannot write, but whose
conversation is unrivalled in its way ;
such insight, such discernment of spirits,
such pure intellectual play, such revolutionary impulses of thought ; whilst he

speaks he has no peer, and yet, all men say, "such partiality of view." I, who hear the same charge always laid at my own gate, do not so readily feel that fault in my friend. But I entreat you to see this man. Since Plato and Plotinus we have not had his like. I have written to Carlyle that he is coming, but have told him nothing about him. For I should like well to set Alcott before that sharp-eyed painter for his portrait, without prejudice of any kind. If A. comes into your neighborhood, he will seek you.

Your picture of England I was very glad to have. It confirms, however, my own impressions. Perhaps you have formed too favorable an opinion of our freedom and receptivity here. And yet I think the most intellectual class of my countrymen look to Germany rather than to England for their recent culture; and Coleridge, I suppose, has always had more readers here than in Britain. . . .

Your friend,   R. W. EMERSON.

VIII. STERLING TO EMERSON.

FALMOUTH, *June 6th*, 1842.

MY DEAR FRIEND, — I have just returned after a two months' absence, forced by ill health to the South. Three weeks in Naples, which I had never seen before, and one in Rome, have renewed a thousand old impressions, given substance to many fancies, and confirmed a faith in ancient Art which has few sharers in this country, but is perhaps as good notwithstanding as some other faiths we know of.

Your letter spiced my welcome home, and must be at once acknowledged. Thanks, and again thanks. Of A. Bronson Alcott I have heard indirectly from London ; and as I must go there soon, I hope to see him there in Carlyle's shadow. It seems too clear that actual England will only a little more than pain and confuse him, — as it does every one not swimming *with* that awful muddy stream of existence which dwindles your Mississippi to a gutter. Very pleasant, however, it will be to hear of this from himself, and still more to find him a real and luminous soul, and not a mere denier and absorbent of the light around.

As to my proceedings you must hear a long story. Since my little volume of poems I have written and published one called the Election, of which a kind of secret was made, partly as a condition of Murray's agreeing to publish it, — otherwise you should have had a copy. It seemed a work to give much offense, but gave none, nobody reading it at all. Besides this, I corrected the printed volume, and rewrote all that appeared in Blackwood of my verses. Also a new poem, a Bernesque satire called Cœur de Lion. Finally, the Tragedy of Strafford, which Carlyle says is trash, but I know not to be that, in spite of certain inevitable faults.

Now all these things are in the hands of Lockhart, of the Quarterly Review, he having proposed to deal with them as if privately printed, and expressing an opinion of them that would have made his article an astonishment to his readers and a comfort to my wife. Thus matters stood when I left, two months ago. I have just written to him to know whether he still designs giving me publicity through his huge trumpet. If, as seems probable, he repents of his dangerous good nature, I shall have no so satisfactory course as to send to you the papers now in his hands, to be used or suppressed at your discretion. Immediately on receiving his answer I will write to inform you of its purport. Whatever he may do, I foresee no chance of being able to print in this country, and shall be most glad to find efficient patronage beyond the Atlantic. Illness and business have as yet stopped any sufficient revision of my prose matters, which, however, I now intend looking into and doctoring.

The pleasantest chance acquaintances of my recent journey were Americans, — a Mr. and Mrs. M—— (he, a lawyer), of Albany. His enjoyment of works of art is, for a man who had never seen any before, really wonderful. My future movements most uncertain, — not pointing, I fear, towards you; perhaps Madeira next winter. . . .

Yours,   JOHN STERLING.

I have said nothing of the painful part of your letter. You will know that I grieve for you and Mrs. Emerson.

IX. STERLING TO EMERSON.

June 13th, 1842.

MY DEAR FRIEND, — Lockhart's illness has prevented him doing anything about my matters. But he still expresses the same decided good will and purpose for the future. Meanwhile I have asked him for the MSS., and shall send you

very soon (probably within a fortnight)
a volume of prose tales, of which the
Onyx Ring is the principal (none of
them new), and about as much verse,
including the Sexton's Daughter, Miscellaneous Poems, and the Election. Of
course I will write with them. But it
may be said now that they must not be
printed among you unless with a fair
prospect of the expenses being paid. No
doubt they are better than a thousand
things that sell largely, but something
in them that would interest you and
other thinkers unfits them for the mul-
titude who have other business than
thinking. At all events, believe me
always yours,

JOHN STERLING.

X. STERLING TO EMERSON.

LONDON, *June 28th*, 1842.

MY DEAR FRIEND, — At last I have
been able to make some progress among
my papers, and am about to despatch a

parcel to you, consisting of two main divisions : the first containing eight Tales, of which the largest and most important is the Onyx Ring ; and the other of five sections of Poems : first, The Sexton's Daughter ; 2, Miscellaneous Poems (those already published in my volume) ; 3, Hymns of a Hermit (greatly altered); 4, Thoughts in Rhyme (corrected) ; 5, The Election. These things, if it be thought worth doing anything with them, might appear either in two small volumes, first verse, second prose, or in one. If I am able to put together a lot of strays and prose thoughts, you shall have them by and by. But as to the whole, I must earnestly beg that you and my other kind friends in America will feel yourselves at perfect liberty to take no further step in the matter.

With my MSS. I shall put up a Tragedy by a friend of mine, which strikes me as singularly fine.

The last fortnight I have been in London in the midst of bustle, but with the great delight of seeing Carlyle, who is more peaceful than I have ever known him. He is immersing himself in Puritanism and Cromwell, — matters with which you Americans have almost a closer connection than we. If he writes our Civil War, the book will have a prodigious advantage over his French Revolution, that there will be one great Egyptian Colossus towering over the temples, tribes, and tents around.

Yesterday, on his table, I found the newspaper report of certain lectures, which, however, I could only glance at. A deep and full phrase that, " The Poet is the man without impediment."

Mr. Alcott has been kind enough to call on me, but I was out (out indeed then), and he would not leave his address. Otherwise *no* engagement would have prevented my finding him.

Thought is leaking into this country,

— even Strauss sells. I hear his copyright is worth more in Germany than that of any living writer, his books selling like Bulwer's novels among us. Some one else has arisen there who attacks Strauss for being too orthodox ; but the Prussian government has taken Strauss under its wing, and forbidden his opponent's books. Forgive this random undiplomatic stuff from

Your affectionate

JOHN STERLING.

XI. STERLING TO EMERSON.

FALMOUTH, *March 29th*, 1843.

MY DEAR FRIEND, — I have for many months been leading a dream-life, fruitful in no result. For a long part of the time I was lying in bed very ill, and indeed, as it seemed, near to death. The prospect was indistinct enough, but far from frightful, and at the worst of the disease it never occurred to me as possible that one's thoughts would terminate with one's pulse. On the whole, though a great deal of time has been quite lost, the experience is worth something. In the last summer, also, I had a long and severe illness. And the upshot seems to me that I must live, if at all, on the terms of the various mythical personages doomed for alternate halves of their year to be lost in Hades. Even the half is more than I can count on in this upper-living air. What uncertainty this gives to all one's projects and arrangements you can well imagine.

In the midst of this confusion, it is some, though rather a melancholy amusement to continue one's lookout over the world, and to see the daily mass of misery, nonsense, and non-consciousness shaping itself into an historic period that will some time or other have its chronicler and heroic singer, and look not quite so beggarly. Of the properly spiritual, England, however, still shows almost as little as the camps of the Barbarians who deluged Rome. Carlyle is our one Man, and he seems to feel it his function, not to build up and enjoy along with his Age, as even a Homer, a Herodotus, could, but to mourn, denounce, and tear in pieces. I find nothing so hard as to discover what effect he really produces. Probably the greater part of his readers find in him only the same sort of mock-turtle nutriment as in Macaulay. Our mechanical civilization, with us as with you, of course, goes on fast enough. The Time spins daily more and bigger teeto-tums with increasing speed and louder hum, and keeps on asking if they be not really celestial orbs, and that the music of the spheres. Of anything much higher, the men of your and my generation, from whom ten years ago I hoped much, seem hardly capable. A good many of them, however, I do think wish for something better than they are able to conceive distinctly, much less to realize.

Of the last age, one respectable relic, you will see, is just removed forever : Southey is dead, with the applause of all good men, but with hardly much deeper feeling from any. Strange proof enough of the want of poems in our language, that he should ever have been held a writer of such. Partly, perhaps, because his works had what one finds in so few English, the greatness of plan and steadiness of execution required for a masterwork, — though these were almost their only merits. I never saw him, and do not much regret it. One living man in Europe whom I should most wish to see is Tieck, — by far, I think, the greatest poet living. His Vittoria Accorambona is well worth your reading. It reproduces in the sixteenth century and in Italy something like the crimson robe, the prophetic slain Cassandra, and the tragic greatness of the Agamemnonian Muse, but this combined at once with

the near meanness and the refined culti-
vation of our modern life.

My own literary matters lie in mag-
netic sleep. Strafford is there finished.
But I have not been able to open it for
many months, and there are a couple of
minor scenes which I fancy I could mend ;
and I can do nothing in the matter till
I look at these, which has not yet been
possible.

In the meanwhile, during my illness,
I have entangled myself in the fancy of
a long Orlandish or Odyssean poem, of
which I have written some eight cantos,
and can promise you at least some amusement from it a hundred and fifty years
hence, by the time England discovers
that it is farther from having a religion
and America a constitution than either
country now supposes.

Believe me with true affection yours,

JOHN STERLING.

CONCORD, *30th June*, 1843.

MY DEAR FRIEND, — I was very sorry
to let the last steamer go to England
without an acknowledgment of your last
letter, whose nobleness under such ad-
verse events had moved my admiration;
but I waited to hear again from ——,
until it was too late. I have twice
charged that amiable but "slow Morti-
mer" to write you himself a report of his
doubts and projects, and I hope he does
so by the packet of to-morrow. Lest he
should not, I will say that I have twice
heard from him since I sent him your
box of printed sheets and MSS. last summer (with my selected list of *imprimenda*),
but both letters expressed a great indeci-
sion as to what he should do. In truth,
our whole foreign-book market has suf-
fered a revolution within eighteen months,
by the new practice of printing whatever
good books or vendible books you send

us, in the cheapest newspaper form, and hawking them in the streets at twelve, eighteen, and twenty-five cents the whole work; and I suppose that —— fears, if his book should prove popular, that it would be pirated at once. I printed Carlyle's Past and Present two months ago, with a preface beseeching all honest men to spare our book; but already a wretched reprint has appeared, published, to be sure, by a man unknown to the Trade, whose wretchedness of type and paper, I have hope, will still give my edition the market for all persons who have eyes and wish to keep them. But, beside the risk of piracy, this cheap system hurts the sale of dear books, or such whose price contains any profit to an author. Add one more unfavorable incident which damped the design, — that a Philadelphia edition of Sterling's Poems was published a year ago, though so ill got up that it did not succeed well, our booksellers think. ——— must be forgiven if he hesitated, but he shall not be forgiven if he do not tell you his own mind. I am heartily sorry that this friendly and pleasing design should have arrived at no better issue. We shall have better news for you one day.

I am touched and stimulated by your heroic mood and labours, so ill as you have been. Please God, you are better now, and, I hope, well. But truly I think it a false standard to estimate health, as the world does, by some fat man, instead of by our power to do our work. If I should lie by whenever people tell me I grow thin and puny, I should lose all my best days. Task these bad bodies and they will serve us and will be just as well a year hence, if they grumble to-day. But in this country this is safer, for we are a nation of invalids. You English are ruddy and robust, and sickness with you is a more serious matter. Yet everything in life looks so differently before and behind, and we reverse our scale of success so often, in our retrospections at our own days and doings, that our estimate of our own health, even, must waver when we see what we have done and gained in the dark hours. I fancy sometimes that I am more practically an idealist than most of my companions ; that I value qualities more and magnitudes less. I must flee to that refuge, too, if I should try to tell you what I have done and do. I have very little to show. Yet my days seem often rich, and I am as easily pleased as my children are. I write a good deal, but it is for the most part without connection, on a thousand topics. Yet I hope, within a year, to get a few chapters ripened into some symmetry and wholeness on the topics that interest all men permanently.

. . . .

Carlyle's new book, which on some accounts I think his best, has given even additional interest to your English practical problem ; and if your conservatism was not so stark, an inertia passing that of Orientalism, the world would look to England with almost hourly expectation of outbreak and revolution. But the world is fast getting English now; and if the old hive should get too warm and crowded, you may circumnavigate the globe without leaving your language or your kindred.

In the hope that my salutations may find you stronger, and strong, and full of good thoughts and good events, I am yours affectionately,

R. W. EMERSON.

XIII. STERLING TO EMERSON.

VENTNOR, I. OF WIGHT,
October 7th, 1843.

MY DEAR FRIEND, — At last on this Saturday evening there is some cessation of the din of workmen, and I can sit down to write to you. The last three months have been all one muddle of carpenters and other materialists, who have hardly left me an hour, and certainly not a day,

quite undisturbed by their practical nonsense.   Now I can draw breath (till Mon-
day morning) in a house which promises
to be as good as a wise man needs, and
far better than most wise men have ever
enjoyed on earth.   It is adjoining a small
new stone-built town, on the south coast,
and close to the sea, and I have some
acres (half a dozen) of field and shrubbery
about me.   One inducement for me is the
shelter and mild climate.   But a thousand
times I have lamented my folly in enga-
ging myself with a pest of improvements,
etc., which has swallowed up all my summer.

Would that I could hope to be re-
warded by such a pleasure as having you
sometime under my thatched roof!   In
the midst of these mechanical arrangements, all higher thoughts have been like
birds in an aviary looking up through
squares of wire that cut across the sky,
whose winged children they imprison.
The birds are there, and the heavens

also, and how little it is, but how insuperable, that divides them! If any good has grown upon me strongly, it is the faith in a Somewhat above all this, — a boat within reach of us at our worst. Every soul on earth, says Mahomet, is born capable of Islam. But you, perhaps, — though having your own difficulties, — hardly know the utter loneliness of a Rational Soul in this England. Except Carlyle, I do not know one man who sees and lives in the idea of a God not exclusively Christian : two or three lads, perhaps ; but every grown man of nobler spirit is either theoretical and lukewarm, or swathed up in obsolete sectarianism.

On Sunday last I had indeed a visit from an old Friend who delighted me by his cordial candour, — John Mill, son of the historian of India, and in many ways notable among us now. His big book on Logic is, I suppose, the highest piece of Aristotelianism that England has brought forth, at all events in our time. How

the sweet, ingenuous nature of the man
has lived and thriven out of his father's
cold and stringent atheism is wonderful
to think, — and most so to me, who during fifteen years have seen his gradual
growth and ripening. There are very
few men in the world on whose generous
affection I should more rely than on his,
whose system seems at first (but only
seems) a Code of Denial.

I was more *struck*, not long ago, by the
mists of one of the most zealous of the
new Oxford School, — like Newman, a
fellow of Oriel, and holding Newman the
first of teachers. Yet this man, who fancies he can blot a thousand years out of
God's Doings, has a zeal, a modesty, a
greatness of soul, that I have hardly
found in more than half a dozen others
on earth. He is, I hear, sometimes half
mad with ill health and low spirits ; a
scholar, a gentleman, a priest, if there is
any true one living, and would let himself
be racked or gibbeted to help any suffer-

ing or erring brother with less self-complacence than most of us feel in giving away a shilling. Strange, is it not, to find Egeria still alive, and in this shape, too, *in fæce Romuli?*

I rejoice that you have something more in store for us; I shall look out eagerly for your lights ahead. Life with me has grown empty and dim enough, and needs what comfort other men's faith is capable of supplying. . . .

   Yours,   JOHN STERLING.

I do not know if the bookseller has sent you a copy of a Ventnor Tragedy which I ventured to decorate with your name.

The Strafford was thus dedicated : —

TO RALPH WALDO EMERSON.

Teacher of starry wisdom high serene,
Receive the gift our common ground supplies ;
Red flowers, dark leaves, that ne'er on earth had been
Without the influence of sidereal skies.

      J. S.

VENTNOR, ISLE OF WIGHT,
 Midsummer Day, 1843.

XIV. EMERSON TO STERLING.

CONCORD, *October 11th*, 1843.

MY DEAR FRIEND, — You have done me an honour to which I have not the least title, and yet it is very dear and animating to me, in putting my name in purple lines before this rich and wise poem of Strafford. I blushed to read, and then thought I should nevermore be unworthy, and these loving words should be an amulet against evil evermore. I might easily mistrust my judgment of the Play in my love of the Poet, and, if you think so, may be wholly wrong, for I read it with lively interest, like a friend's manuscript, from end to end, and grew prouder and richer in my friend with every scene. The subject is excellent, so great and eventful a crisis, and each of the figures in that history filled and drunk with a national idea, and with such antagonism as makes them colossal, and adds solemnity and omens to their words and actions. I was glad to find the Countess of Carlisle in poetry, whom I had first learned to know by that very lively sketch from Sir Toby Matthew, which I read in one of Forster's Lives. I do not yet know whether the action of the piece is sufficiently stout and irresistible, alarming and victimizing the reader after the use of the old " purifiers ; " it seems to me, as I hastily read, managed with judgment and lighted with live coals; but I am quite sure of the dense and strong sentences whose energy and flowing gentleness at the same time give the authentic expression of health and perfect manhood.

I rejoice when I remember in what sickness and interruption, by your own account, this drama had its elaboration and completion. As soon as I had read it once, Margaret Fuller, our genius and Muse here, and a faithful friend of yours, seized the book peremptorily and carried it away, so that I am by no means master of its contents. Meantime, may the just honour of all the best in Old and in New England cherish the poem and the Poet. Send me, I pray you, better news of your health than your last letter contained. I observe that you date from the Isle of Wight. Two letters (one from —— and one from me) went to your address in Falmouth, in the course of the last summer, which I hope, for the exculpation of your friends here, you received.

I am, I think, to sit fast at home this winter coming, and arrange a heap of materials that much and wide scribbling has collected. I shall probably send this letter by Mr. James, a man who adds to many merits the quality of being a good friend of both you and me, and who, proposing with his family to spend a winter in England, for health and travel, thinks he has a right to see you. He is at once so manly, so intelligent, and so ardent that I have found him excellent company. The highest and holiest Muse dwell with you always.

Yours affectionately,

R. W. EMERSON.

My friend and near neighbor, W. Ellery Channing (a nephew of the late Dr. C.), desires me to send you his little volume of poems. I love Ellery so much as to have persuaded myself long since that he is a true poet, if these lines should not show it. Read them with as much love in advance as you can. Mr. J. will bring them.

XV. EMERSON TO STERLING.

CONCORD, *October 15th*, 1843.

MY DEAR STERLING, — Henry James, of New York, a man of ingenious and liberal spirit, and a chief consolation to me when I visit his city, proposes to spend a winter in England with his family, for his health and other benefit, and desires to see you, for whom he has

77

much affection. I am quite sure that I shall serve you both by sending him to you. Yours,

R. W. EMERSON.

XVI. EMERSON TO STERLING.

CONCORD, 31st January, 1844.

MY DEAR FRIEND, — The mercury has been at zero at my door, with little variation, for more than a week. Boston harbour is frozen up for six miles down to the forts, yet the newspapers tell me this morning that the merchants have resolved to saw through these miles a passage for your royal steamer and other sea-going ships to-morrow, and I must not wait another hour if I would speed my good wishes to the Isle of Wight.

By an unhappy chance, the January Dials did not sail as they ought in last month's steamer, and you should receive by this, *via* London and Carlyle, a copy of No. XV., which contains a critique, written by Margaret Fuller, on Strafford,

and other children of genius, both yours
and other men's. I heartily hope you
will find something right and wise in my
friend's judgments, if with something in-
adequate, and if her pen ramble a little.
It was her own proposition to write the
piece, led by her love both of you and of
me. After she began it, she decided to
spread her censure so wide, and com-
prise all dramas as well as Strafford.
She was full of spirits in her undertak-
ing, but, unhappily, the week devoted to
its performance was exanimated, may I
say, by cruel aches and illness, and she
wrote me word that she was very sorry,
but the piece was ruined. However, as
you are by temper and habit such a cos-
mopolitan, I hope one day you shall see
with eyes my wise woman, hear her with
ears, and see if you can escape the virtue
of her enchantments. She has a sultry
Southern nature, and Corinna never can
write.

I learned by your last letter that you

had builded a house, and I glean from Russell all I can of your health and aspect; and as James is gone to your island, I think to come still nearer to you through his friendly and intelligent eyes. Send me a good gossiping letter, and prevent all my proxies. What can I tell you to invite such retaliation? I dwell with my mother, my wife, and two little girls, the eldest five years old, in the midst of flowery fields. I wasted much time from graver work in the last two months in reading lectures to Lyceums far and near; for there is now a "lyceum," so called, in almost every town in New England, and, if I would accept every invitation, I might read a lecture every night. My neighbors in this village of Concord are Ellery Channing, who sent his poems to you, a youth of genius; Thoreau, whose name you may have seen in the Dial; and Hawthorne, a writer of tales and historiettes, whose name you may not have seen, though he too prints books. All these three persons are superior to their writings, and therefore not obnoxious to Kant's observation, "Detestable is the company of literary men."

Good as these friends are, my habit is so solitary that we do not often meet. My literary or other tasks accomplished are too little to tell. I do not know how it happens, but there are but seven hours, often but five, in an American scholar's day; the twelve, thirteen, fifteen, that we have heard of, in German libraries, are fabulous to us. Probably in England you find a mean between Massachusetts and Germany. The performances of Goethe, the performances of Scott, appear superhuman to us in their quantity, let alone their quality. Sometimes I dream of writing the only historical thing I know, — the influence of old Calvinism, now almost obsolete, upon the education of the existing generation in New England. I am quite sure, if it could be truly done, it would be new to your people, and a valuable memorandum to ours.

I have lately read George Sand's Consuelo, of which the first volume pleased me mightily, the others much less, and yet the whole book shows an extraordinary spirit. The writer apprehends the force of simplicity of behaviour, and enjoys, how greatly, the meeting of two strong natures. But I have gossiped to the end of my line, and so do commend myself affectionately to you.

R. W. EMERSON.

XVII. STERLING TO EMERSON.

VENTNOR, *February 20th*, 1844.

MY DEAR FRIEND, — I had proposed a letter to you as this morning's work, and now down the throat of my purpose jumps your own of January 31. Long since I ought to have thanked you for the previous one, but have been too sick and sad.[1] Your reception of Strafford

[1] During the year Sterling's mother and wife had died

was a great pleasure, — so far as anything is so now. The work has become altogether distant and distasteful to me, but I can enjoy your kindness. I got from an English bookseller the October Dial, which is pleasant reading. If one could have the whole of the former numbers it would be good for me, but I own that, except your own doings, there is little in it that comes home. Channing, I suppose, I must thank for his friendly gift ; but the volume — perhaps from my own deadness — gave me little true comfort. It seemed to show abundant receptivity, but of productivity little. Everything can too easily be referred to some other parent. If he would read diligently the correspondence of Schiller and Goethe, he would learn much, and would either cease to be a poet or become a good one. At least one hopes so. That book has

within three days. Sorrowful and sick, he had moved with his six children, two of them infants, to his last earthly home, the house in Ventnor.

to me greater value than any or all those on the theory of art, — besides the beautiful, mild, and solid humanity which it displays in every word. There are hardly perhaps three Englishmen living with the slightest thought of what Art is, — the unity and completeness of the Ideal. The crowd, when weary of themselves and their own noisy choking Reality, take refuge in Fiction, but care not how lazy, coarse, and empty. The few among us who look higher, generally the young, seem satisfied, not with the Ideal, but their own feelings and notions about it, which they substitute for the thing itself; sermons on the Incarnation instead of the Incarnate God. Hence all the dreamy Shelleyan rhapsodies and rhetorical Wordsworthian moralizings. But who seriously strives to create images? Who does not waste himself in hunting shadows, forgetting that you cannot have them without first getting the substance, and that with it you can never be in want of them?

So it stands with us in England: is it otherwise in America? I fear not. Tennyson does better, but does little, and they say will hardly wake out of tobacco smoke into any sufficient activity. Carlyle, our far greater Tacitus, in truth hates all poetry except for that element in it which is not poetic at all, and aims at giving a poetic completeness to historic fact. He is the greatest of moralists and politicians, a gigantic anti-poet. As far as I know, there is not a man besides, on either side of the Atlantic, writing in English, either in prose or verse, who need be spoken of.

. . . .

Your friend James pleased me well. Would that he could have stayed here longer and let me know more of him! But after all regrets, Life is good, — to see the face of Truth, and enjoy the beauty of tears and smiles, and know one's self a man, and love what belongs to manhood, — all this is a blessing that may console us for all wants, and *that* sickness and sorrow, and, one may trust, Death, cannot take away. Yet I wish I could have talk with you some day.

I am yours,

JOHN STERLING.

This is a miserable scrap to send in the track of Columbus and Raleigh. But I have been too ill in body, and am still too sad in mind.

XVIII. STERLING TO EMERSON.

VENTNOR, I. OF WIGHT, *June 14th*, 1844.

MY DEAR FRIEND, — Perhaps you may have heard that for the last three months I have been a dying man. It is certain that I never can recover. But there seems a melancholy possibility that I may have to drag on a year or two of helplessness, cut off from all society and incapable of any exertion. It is a case for submission,

but hardly for thankfulness. The begin-
ning of the illness was a violent and extensive bleeding from the lungs, of which,
however, I have had prelibations for many
years. It was strange to see the thick
crimson blood pouring from one's own
mouth while feeling hardly any pain ; ex-
pecting to be dead in five minutes, and
noticing the pattern of the room-paper
and of the Doctor's waistcoat as compos-
edly as if the whole had been a dream.

At present I am quite incapable, as
indeed I was when I wrote last, of sending you anything worth your reading.

.   .   .   .

On both sides of Eternity (the *out*
and *in*),

   Your affectionate

     JOHN STERLING.

XIX. EMERSON TO STERLING.

CONCORD, *5th July*, 1844.

MY DEAR FRIEND, — What news you
send me, — how dark and bitter, and how

87

unlooked for, and so firmly and soldierly
told! I got your letter yesterday, and in
it the first hint I have had of this disaster.
I dream of you and of Carlyle, whenever
steamers go or come, but easily omit to
write; and this is the punishment of my
luxury, that you should be threatened,
and I should know nothing of your danger and mine. I cling now to the hope
you show me that these symptoms may
not be so grave or of so instant sequel as
their first menace. Yesterday I thought
I would go to England, and see you alive;
it seemed practicable and right. But the
same hour showed inextricable engage-
ments here at home, and I could not see
your manly strength, which is so dear to
me, and I might easily make injurious de-
mands on a sick man. You are so brave
you must be brave for both of us, and
suffer me to express the pain I feel at
these first tidings. I shall come soon
enough to general considerations which
will weigh with you, and with me, I sup-

pose, to reduce this calamity within the sphere. I, who value nothing so much as *character* in literary works, have believed that you would live to enjoy the slow, sure homage of your contemporaries to the valor and permanent merits of your Muse; and I have pleased myself how deeply with a certain noble emulation in which widely separated friends would bear each other in constant regard, and with months and years augment the benefit each had to confer. This must now be renounced, and the grand words I hear and sometimes use must be verified, and I must think of that which you represent, and not of the representative beloved. Happy is it whilst the Blessed Power keeps unbroken the harmony of the inward and the outward, and yields us the perfect expression of good in a friend! But if it will disunite the power and the form, the power is yet to be infinitely trusted, and we must try, unwilling, the harsh grandeurs of the spiritual nature. Each of us more readily faces the issue alone than on the account of his friend. We find something dishonest in learning to live without friends : whilst death wears a sublime aspect to each of us. God send you, my dear brother, the perfect mind of truth and heart of love, however the event is to fall ! Thousands of hearts have owed to you the finest mystic influences: I must and will believe in happy reactions which will render to you the most soothing music at unawares.

.   .   .   .

If you have strength, write me, if only your name. But I shall continue to hope to see your face. And so I love you and I thank you, dear Friend !

Yours,   R. WALDO EMERSON.

XX. STERLING TO EMERSON.

HILLSIDE, VENTNOR, *August 1st,* 1844.

MY DEAR FRIEND, — I am very ill to-day, but, as I am likely to be worse rather than better, I make the effort of.

writing a few words to thank you for your letter, and also for your care about my papers.

.   .   .   .

You and I will never meet in this world. Among my friends you are an Unseen One, but not the less valued. Heaven help you to realize all your inspirations. They will be a blessing to many as well as yourself. My struggle, I trust, is nigh over. At present it is a painful one. But I fear nothing, and hope much.

Your affectionate and grateful

JOHN STERLING.

CONCLUSION

IN the last days of September Carlyle wrote to tell Emerson of the death of their friend ; how calm he had been, and brave, and how to the very last he worked alone, setting his house in order and sending farewells to his friends, whom he preferred not to see. He tells how Sterling's brother, arriving after a short absence on the last evening of his life, "found no visible change, the brave Patient calm as ever, ready to speak as ever, — to say, in direct words which he would often do, or indirectly as his whole speech and conduct did, 'God is Great.' Anthony and he talked for a while, then took leave for the night; in a few minutes more, Anthony was summoned to the bedside, and at eleven o'clock, as I

said, the curtain dropt, and it was all
ended. — *Enge !*

.   .   .   .

" Our Friend is buried in Ventnor
Churchyard ; four big Elms overshadow
the little spot ; it is situated on the
southeast side of that green Island, on
the slope of steep hills (as I understand
it) that look toward the Sun, and are
close within sight and hearing of the
Sea. There shall he rest, and have fit
lullaby, this brave one. He has died as
a man should ; like an old Roman, yet
with the Christian Bibles and all newest
revelations present to him. He refused
to see friends, men whom I think he
loved as well as any, — me for one when
I obliquely proposed it, he refused. He
was even a little stern on his nearest re-
latives when they came to him : Do I
need your help to die ? Phocion-like he
seemed to feel degraded by physical de-
cay ; to feel that he ought to wrap his

mantle round him, and say, 'I come, Persephoneia; it is not I that linger!'"

In the answering letter, written from Concord on the last day of the year, Emerson said : —

"Your two letters containing tidings, the first of the mortal illness, and the second of the death of Sterling, I had no heart to answer. I had nothing to say. Alas! as in so many instances heretofore, I knew not what to think. Life is somewhat customary and useful ; and death is the unusual and astonishing ; it kills in so far the survivor also, when it ravishes from him friendship and the most noble and admirable qualities. That which we call faith seems somewhat stoical and selfish, if we use it as a retreat from the pangs this ravishment inflicts. I had never seen him, but I held him fast ; now I see him not, but I can no longer hold him. Who can say what he yet is and will be to me?"

CONCLUSION

Carlyle's verdict on his friend's life, in his "Memoir," is that it was "a tragedy; high hopes, noble efforts; under thickening difficulties and impediments, ever new nobleness of valiant effort; and the result death with conquests by no means corresponding." But even while he is writing this dismal summary, the beauty and help that this short life had for those who saw and felt it, and for those who should later consider it, sweeps over him, and, the human heart breaking through the crust, he admits its claim, and more, the call of Nature, and thus ends : —

"The history of this long-continued prayer and endeavour, lasting in various figures for near forty years, may now and for some time coming have something to say to men!

"Nay, what of men, or of the world? Here, visible to myself for some while, was a brilliant human presence, distinguishable, honourable and lovable amid the dim, common populations ; among the million little beautiful, once more a beautiful human soul, whom I, among others, recognized and lovingly walked with, while the years and the hours were. Sitting now by his tomb in thoughtful mood, the new times bring a new duty for me. 'Why write a Life of Sterling?' I imagine I had a commission higher than the world's, — the dictate of Nature herself, to do what is now done. *Sic prosit.*"